IDEAS IN

Guilt

Kalu Singh

Series editor: Ivan Ward

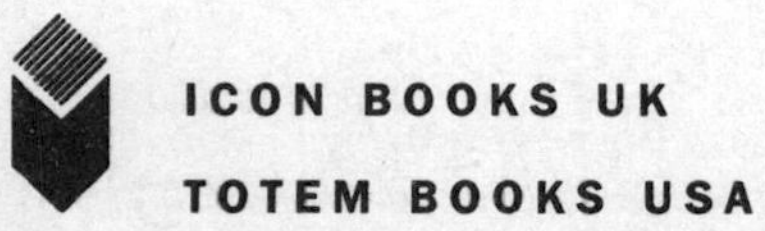

Published in the UK in 2000
by Icon Books Ltd., Grange Road,
Duxford, Cambridge CB2 4QF
email: info@iconbooks.co.uk
www.iconbooks.co.uk

Published in the USA in 2001
by Totem Books
Inquiries to: Icon Books Ltd.,
Grange Road, Duxford,
Cambridge CB2 4QF, UK

Distributed in the UK, Europe,
Canada, South Africa and Asia
by the Penguin Group:
Penguin Books Ltd.,
27 Wrights Lane,
London W8 5TZ

In the United States,
distributed to the trade by
National Book Network Inc.,
4720 Boston Way, Lanham,
Maryland 20706

Published in Australia in 2000
by Allen & Unwin Pty. Ltd.,
PO Box 8500, 9 Atchison Street,
St. Leonards, NSW 2065

Library of Congress catalog
card number applied for

Series editor: Ivan Ward

ISBN 1 84046 190 X

Typesetting by Hands Fotoset

Printed and bound in the UK by
Cox & Wyman Ltd., Reading

Introduction

Imagine a world without guilt. Imagine a life, your life, without guilt. What do you feel right now? Puzzlement, fear, relief, hope, desire, joy, release – or perhaps even shame; but I hope not guilt. That would be the world's end, wouldn't it?

Try again. Try these words:

I refuse to feel guilty. Guilt is a destructive emotion and doesn't fit in with my Life Plan. [1]

Guilt is petit bourgeois crap. An artist creates his own moral universe.[2]

The first quotation is from the feckless Adrian Mole, responding to a crisis with typically pointless bravado. It is one of Woody Allen's fictional creations who makes the second remark, but after quoting it, biographer Marion Meade comments:

Woody was about to find out that playing by his own rules would cost him millions in legal fees, the loss of his children, and abandonment by his audience.[3]

But what is guilt? Is it a sensation or a thought, or a medium for sensation and thought? Or a something, a force, sometimes internal, sometimes external, that is beyond thought and sensation? Most commonly, people say that guilt 'gnaws', capturing the sense of something inside and inaccessible, attacking one relentlessly. Or it is a burden that one can never shake off. There may be other metaphors: that it is like a pebble in one's shoe, a chafing thong, a polyp, leaking silicone, a throbbing phantom limb, a torn disabling gene, an irregularly beating transplanted pig's heart, a skin graft that tears and becomes septic, Dorian Gray's picture, the pall of volcanic ash.

Psychoanalysis takes up the challenge to heal guilt. Theology and its bastard aspect – organised religion – are outraged at the temerity of psychoanalysis to encroach upon its fiefdom. Surely all one needs to know about guilt – how to define it, explain it, contain it and heal it – is given within the paradigm of theology? How can there be non-religious guilt? Perhaps since the Renaissance, and certainly since the Enlightenment, this has been the paradox: that religion has failed in its promise to alleviate guilt – the guilt it had created in order to demonstrate the faith's power by healing it. The only remaining excuse is the perennial plea of the tension between the perfection of the theology and the culpability of the believers. But from the psychoanalytic point of view, clients arrive at the therapeutic realm variously crippled by guilts which religion has failed to heal, even if it didn't create them. Religion has had two to seven millennia, depending on your religion, to perfect its theology and its technique: psychoanalysis has had one century.

Ruling Passions: The Inheritance

'Guilt' is a concept that forms part of a matrix to do with moral division and reunion: 'transgression', 'fault', 'accusation', 'blame', 'plea', 'shame', 'contrition', 'remorse', 'repentance', 'apology', 'punishment', 'revenge', 'forgiveness', 'reparation', 'reconciliation'.

The typical narrative instantiating the above matrix begins with a morally capable and responsible person intending and performing an act which transgresses a rule or law – moral, civil or criminal – of the community which has defined itself partly by the instituting of those rules and laws, and among whom he lives. Ideally, the laws and rules were the product of the free dialogue of free citizens, and their purpose was to facilitate the free development of all. The purpose of the panoply of concepts listed above is to reintegrate the individual who through the transgression has separated himself from his community. The matrix can stand unvarnished by the religious and theological gloss with which it is usually associated. In the Christian revelation, the morally capable person carries from birth the stain of Original Sin. Though this is sometimes referred to as a *felix culpa* (happy fault), because it induced in God the compassion of the Incarnation, the doctrine demands a limitless fountain of individual guilt as part of the necessary mortal repentance. Perhaps the Judaic curse of 'visiting the iniquities of the fathers upon the children unto the third and fourth generation'[4] was attenuated somewhat by this new gospel, but it was also used by Christian states to justify anti-Semitism.

'There should be a statute of limitations . . . why do you keep breaking our balls for that crime?', began a sketch by the American satirist Lenny Bruce, on the Law, which hounded him to death. 'Why, Jew, because you skirt the issue. You blame it on the Roman soldiers.' 'Alright. I'll clear the air once and for all. Yes, we did it. I did it, my family. I found a note in my basement. It said: "We killed him. Signed Morty."'[5]

This sketch seems facetious, even puerile. But a glance at the history of the Diaspora, let alone the horrors of the last century, reminds us how much ache and rage is in such humour. By a curious symmetry, many Jews remain outraged that the Catholic church, despite lavish Papal gestures of apology, still won't come clean about its culpability in the Holocaust.

Guilt seems so absolutely a personal, individual emotion that it seems difficult to talk about 'institutional guilt' or 'State guilt'. There is of course institutional failure and institutional culpability, whether by local-civic or international standards. But whereas in personal guilt there may be a crippling emotional cost to the individual, in institutional guilt there may be an economic cost of compensation, which is differently crippling. Hence the tobacco industry's decades-long guilty evasion of the apposite word 'addiction', or the London Metropolitan Police's guilty hesitation about imputing racist motives to criminals or themselves.

Out of the Holocaust came a re-examination of the familiar concepts of 'collective guilt' or 'guilt-by-association' – the shadow of the criminals; and the sharpest delineation of the rarer concept of 'survivor guilt' – the shadow of the victims. No secular citizen – and, I conjecture, almost no believer – would want Germans or Jews or Roma (the world's gypsies) yet to be born, to come into the world in 2100 under either of these shadows. But ascribing guilt even to those of that fatal generation is fraught with controversy, as the author of *Hitler's Willing Executioners* found.[6] Within the concept of 'survivor-guilt' there is, in addition to the ordinary layers of mourning and grief (here heightened by historical exigencies), the terrifying guilt that one's survival 'proves' that one failed as a human being to rescue those who died.

We are living through a period of re-examination, in philosophy and politics, of the concept of 'the bystander', both at the State level – as we saw in Kosovo in 1999 – and at the civic level. The moral ambiguities of the latter were wonderfully opened in the final episode of that masterpiece of situation comedy, *Seinfeld*. Stranded in 'Sticksville', the amoral, urban quartet witness a robbery. They can see only the comedic value in the victim's suffering. A local policeman observes their response and arrests them for breaking the new Good Samaritan Law, '[which] requires you to help or assist anyone in danger, as long as it is reasonable to do so'. Their Defence Counsel argues: 'You cannot be a bystander and be guilty. They want to create a whole new animal – the guilty bystander!'[7] But as the very title of the new law testifies, even these modern ambiguities seem unable to step from under the shadow of Biblical models.

The last tired punches between the combatants of the Reformation and the Counter-Reformation can be seen in the aphorism: 'Catholics have a sense of guilt, but no sense of sin. Protestants have a sense of sin but no sense of guilt. So it is that Catholics enjoy their sinning more than Protestants, who aren't allowed to enjoy anything.'[8] Jews and Buddhists would probably laugh at both for their casuistry and vain religiosity. Of course, both Christian denominations have an astigmatic concept of sin, focusing more on sexuality than avarice and wrath; most children would be surprised to learn that there are as many cardinal sins as there are Disney dwarves. The bathetic dimension to the casting of their mighty shadows on psychological development can be seen from the fact of the recent Catholic revaluation of the ordinary, albeit subversively named, activity of 'bashing the bishop' or, in the gender-blind phrase, 'making glue without boiling a horse'.[9] Just think how much emotion and thought, how many billions and billions of hours, have been wasted by men and women, priests and the laity, over two millennia, trying to manage the doctrinal guilt over masturbation. It's not that the Church has recently acquired a new scientific fact: more a belated gesture of compassion.

Can Fuck, Won't Cook: Freud's Account of Guilt

Sigmund Freud was aware of this inheritance, and especially of the wealth of narratives of fault-guilt-reconciliation in parable and literature. What did he imagine he could add to these 'explanations' of the human experience of guilt? Because he saw himself as a kind of hybrid between an ancient, questing hero and a modern detective, we might begin with some ordinary stories and the question: 'What kind and level of guilt do the following protagonists display?'

i. A woman runs into a room, straightens the tablecloth and rings for the maid. When the maid comes she sends her away instantly, though while they are briefly together she draws the maid's attention, silently and without accusation, to a stain on the tablecloth. She does this several times a day.

ii. A man walking in the country accidentally kicks a pebble into the middle of the road. He pauses, and then moves the stone from the road. But then he pauses again, and this time he returns the stone to where his first kick had taken it.

iii. A respectable person, during the course of an analysis in which he has appeared anxious, commits a pointless crime; and despite the possibility of punishment – in fact, partly because of its likelihood – he feels a tremendous sense of relief.

iv. A woman goes on and on, and quite shamelessly on and on, saying how depressed she is. Why?

Freud was deeply sceptical of the ability of received rationality to describe what was happening in such stories – what they revealed about human desire, thought and action. The facts of ambiguity and complexity in human relations are signalled by language itself, by the ambiguity present in modal verbs. 'Can' is used for ability and for request; 'may' for probability as well as permission; 'will/shall' for intention, prediction and obligation. Thus the title of this section, my seemingly trivial gloss on an evocative example that even Freud characterised as 'absurd':

A maidservant refuses to go on cooking because her master has started a love-affair with her.[10]

The attempts of neurotics and obsessives and psychotics to manage the negotiations with the real or imagined forces and entities setting these ambiguous meanings, *viz.* parents, teachers, angels and devils, is marked by such hesitations and confusions of language.

Freud too began with ordinary notions of 'instinct', 'impulse', 'emotion', 'anxiety', 'pressure', as he attempted to explain the everyday experiences of pleasure and of sickness, and hence of guilt. One of his greatest achievements was to redefine the temporal scope and characteristics of human sexuality. With respect to time, he posits a sequence beginning with infantile sexuality, transmuting to an asexual/latency period and then a pubescent efflorescence enduring well past capability to death. To this characteristic of antiquity he added not only the imperiousness and proneness to maldevelopment – recognised, in their own terms, by all religions – but also plasticity: its capacity to become something else.

Freud sought to show how psychic energy becomes the entities necessary for its management. The Id with its reservoir of instinctual energy (libido/Eros/someforce) first bodying forth, somehow, the Ego; and that in turn bodying forth the Superego. However the instinctual forces are conceived – whether *endosomatic* like hunger or *endopsychic* like love – their conflict generates four levels of developmental organisation: oral, anal, phallic and genital. Each phase articulates a kind of thinking: libidinous scopophilia (must see) becomes the more monastic epistemophilia (must know). The more familiar equation of knowledge, sexualised vision and guilt is demonstrated in the Edenic tale.

The basic developmental tasks at the cognitive level are, first, to distinguish between the affect and the idea of an instinct; and second, between the unconscious primary processes and the secondary processes, waking thought and judgement. A baby's awareness of the affect/emotion attending her awareness of hunger is modified by her learning to name and recognise the concept/idea 'hunger'. But the pressure of the affect can sometimes mobilise unconscious processes which tend towards a hallucinatory fulfilment of the instincts. As Theseus observes in Shakespeare's *A Midsummer Night's Dream*:

Such tricks hath strong imagination,
That, if it would but apprehend some joy,
It comprehends some bringer of that joy.
(V, i, 18–20)

It is by the reality testing conducted by the secondary processes that the individual attains to real and predictable fulfilment; although, as Freud was at pains to emphasise, the requirements of civilisation, the embodiment of the collective's understanding of the secondary processes, are a neurosis-level inducing deferment of gratification. The sense of frustration at this deferment leads to intermittent hatred of the frustrator, be it the parent, the educators or the police – in fact, anyone who threatens the consolations of narcissism.

We now have enough forces, or concepts of them, to tell the developmental story at the macro/human rather than micro/endo level. At the heart of Freud's theoretical edifice is the Oedipus complex, so let us now look at this mighty story.

Unwittingly, King Oedipus kills his father and marries his mother. Before the songwriter Prince, he is the proto-'sexy motherfucker'. From this sublime Sophoclean tragedy, and perhaps Jocasta's generalisation, 'Many a man before you, in his dreams, has shared his mother's bed' (*Oedipus Rex*, ll. 1074–5), Freud constructed a developmental psychodrama.

A boy-baby's first experiences are of his mother's

absolute availability to him, to satisfy all his desires. Then comes the experience of the partial withdrawal of this availability. When he understands that his mother is dividing her attention between him and his father, he feels rage, and imagines removing or killing his father and once again having his mother all to himself. (Look at a kid at solitary play, punching and kicking the air – he seems to be forever fighting imaginary adversaries.) But when the boy sees clearly the disparity between himself and his father, their penis sizes and their strengths, he realises the futility of his wish. This despair is worsened by an anxiety that his father has discovered his wish and may annihilate him first. The resolution of these terrors comes with the awareness of his father's love for him, his understanding that one day he will be as strong as his father, and that by the eternal relinquishment of his desire for his mother he will be able to have some sort of unthreatened relationship with her and his father – and probably a mother-like woman of his own, eventually. The internalisation of the prohibition of the wish, and the attendant fear of punishment, is the instituting of the Superego, the community line of guilt.

What of girl-babies? Here is another story. A woman is forced by 'the Gods' to send away her husband, but is allowed to keep her child by him. In their household she brings up the girl, barely seeing her for the shadow she bears of her absent husband. The girl grows up into a beautiful young woman: talented, but deeply troubled by the burden of the pasts of others. One day, her father returns to visit them both. Though he now has a new wife in another town, he sleeps with his first wife. His daughter is puzzled – she doesn't know if she is upset. But she does know the moment he kisses her at their parting, as he parts her lips to bring his tongue into her mouth, that two things have suddenly happened: she has flamed into being, she is visible; and she can see herself burning.

They begin a secret, sexual relationship, meeting in the caves of the mountain deserts. Eventually her mother begins to suspect, and when the daughter seems to taunt her with a careless confidence, she drags her to the 'Oracle'. But such is the daughter's desire and cunning, even the 'Sybil' is fooled. The daughter sees her mother broken by this utter humiliation. For a moment she feels an absolute, god-like triumph – and in the next instant, utter desolation and bereavement.

My performance is so good that I'm frightened. . . . The doctor [psychiatrist] looks at me sitting before him in my vulgar dress, and he believes me. I know it, and so does my mother. He's mine, not hers, and so I have what I wanted – what I thought I wanted. She is alone. I've taken her husband and now her only ally, the one person with whom she can share her troubles. . . . And I, I begin to know the misery of wounding the person I love most.[11]

This is a true story – hence 'doctor' and not 'Sybil' – from Kathryn Harrison's astonishing Elektral autobiography, *The Kiss* (1997). Perhaps *the* Oedipal story was also true. Either, and both, ought to be sufficient proof of the heuristic value Freud makes of it, but I guess anti-Freudians will still quibble. In Harrison's life, unlike the Greek, phantasy is intentionally made actual, and the reservoirs of anxiety and desire that feed the Oedipus complex would seem to have been alleviated and satiated by achievement. But of course they haven't. The sense of guilt has been made infinitely more intense and unmanageable, inducing almost suicidal desperation. Freud concluded that this ineluctable psychodrama forms the developmental trajectory of all mortals, and the residues of anxiety and desire – some billion shades of guilt – that are deposited by whatever inevitable misnegotiation of it an individual manages, are carried forward into adult life, being displaced on all future relationships. The 'drama' is further complicated by Freud's belief that human nature is inherently bisexual – the child wants to be and have BOTH parents – and thus 'the idea of regarding every sexual act as a process in which four persons are involved'.[12] This complex is the defining contribution of psychoanalysis to the account of guilt. Some may see this structural, developmental guilt as an atheistic correlate to the Fall, when sexuality, knowledge and death enter the world as the defining parameters of human consciousness.

In what way might this idea help us to make sense of the four stories, or rather case histories, above? Please turn back to pages 11–12 and refresh your memories!

The Running Wife

This poor woman, many years earlier, had had a disastrous wedding night. Her 'very much older' husband couldn't. He tried all night, 'many times . . . running from his room into hers', but failed all night. In the morning he said angrily, 'I should feel ashamed in front of the housemaid'; so he got some red ink and spilled it on the sheets. In his ignorance, or perhaps just pathetic nervousness, he spilled it in the wrong place![13]

In the 'ritual' of the present there is not the former triangle of husband-wife-maid, but only the wife 'showing' the maid the stain on the tablecloth. Freud interprets this gesture as arising from the wife's anxiety to reassure her husband that he wasn't (always) impotent. But not only is he not there; the couple have been separated for years. So his wife is attending to (or trying to manage), in the present, an affect attached to a very old experience. I would suggest that the obliqueness of the communication might also arise out of her sense of guilt at her disappointment, contempt, even rage at her inadequate ex-husband. Freud, the son of a much-younger wife, doesn't pick up on the age difference and whether Elektral tensions and guilts had inhibited their mutual desires. Who was the husband's angry 'should' for, really?

In a scenario where lust is mutual and allowable, the woman might want to preserve HER reputation. When Ovid fails to make the idiot stand, his mistress Corinna splashes her face with water before leaving the bedroom, so that her maid will think she has had a steamy time.[14]

What did the maid symbolise for this class – the family's informal press-secretary to the neighbourhood, an embodied conscience, or the necessary conduit/sewer of other people's sexuality? One thinks of Kafka, at 33, still fascinated and revolted by the 'evidence' of his parents' sexuality:

At home the sight of the double bed, of sheets that have been slept in, of nightshirts carefully laid out, can bring me to the point of retching, can turn my stomach inside out; it is as though my birth had not been final, as though from this fusty life I keep being born again and again in this fusty room; as though I had to return there for confirmation, being – if not quite, at least in part – indissolubly connected with these distasteful things . . . the primeval slime.[15]

He passed them thousands of times to get to his room, but in a sense he never got past them at all. There are few literary geniuses whose sexuality was as guiltily 'fucked up' as Kafka's. He only managed to leave the nest to starve and die. Out of his private hell of an irreparable sense of separation from and longing for the love of his parents, came his many masterpieces of the protean terrors of not-quite-placeable guilt.

The Stoned Man

The young man makes a random, unintended move – he kicks a stone into the road. He then imagines a coincidence – his fiancée's carriage hitting that stone. He further imagines a (near) fatal consequence of the impact of these two bodies, stone and coach wheel; and his beloved broken, even dead. This last may not have been pictured, but the thought induces in him a series of sensations – anxiety, guilt, shame and fear – to which we will return. In response to these, and in order to lessen the distress, the unpleasure, they have caused (Freud uses the word 'obliged' to describe the motive), he goes to the stone, picks it up, and places it 'out of the way'. One possibility is instantly obviated: an object connected with him coming into fatal contact with an object connected to his fiancée. But then the same feelings – anxiety, shame, guilt and fear – return. They are the same, but in some strangely different way. He decides to put the stone back. This brings greater relief, but unsurprisingly only for a while.[16]

Freud suggests that his decision to remove the

stone, based as it is on an irrational interpretation of the possibility of an accident, discloses a barely conscious awareness of an impulse to commit violence upon his fiancée; so removing the stone protects her from this impulse of his. But in undoing that protection, by returning the stone, he is reclaiming, again in a barely conscious way, a right to that impulse. In the first gesture there is the perfect paradox of impotence: a tiny pebble is imagined as being capable of overturning the coach. At the symbolic level, the man is obviously the stone: he, or his impulse to violence, is a knot of badness like a stone, which could be sufficiently destructive of the woman he also loves and needs. A woman in a coach is also a powerful symbol of wombs and children, and as Melanie Klein saw, in children's play, sex is sometimes imagined as a brutal collision. The other aspect of the man-as-stone is that of the crushed, perhaps emasculated, person's sense of omnipotence – I feel like a pebble, but I am really a monolith. The defence is strong enough to release some energy of concern for the fiancée, to protect her from himself, and so he removes the stone. But the inadequacy of this response is revealed by the distress which ceases only when he returns the stone. But what does this mean, this acceptance of the tentative irruption of malice towards his fiancée? Is this the price for the recovery of a sufficient sense of the Reality Principle to realise two facts, one from physics – that tiny pebbles can't overturn coaches – and one from grammar and logic – that might (possibility) doesn't entail must (necessity)? Or perhaps not so much 'price' as 'partial benefit'. He has arrived, on the road, at an awareness of seemingly intolerable ambivalence: he partly loves and partly hates his fiancée. In his therapy he learns how to tolerate such ambivalence as ordinary life.

The Good Criminal

With the tale of the patient who feels relief after committing a seemingly pointless crime, we have the experiential and theoretical limiting case. In a fragment entitled 'Criminals From a Sense of Guilt', Freud considers the burden of guilt which is felt to be so boundless, so timeless and enduring that it feels unnameable and thus unthinkable, that it can find palliation, albeit brief, only in a present, tangible, codeable transgression that will bring certain guilt and possible punishment.[17] This Absolute-Guilt, Freud conjectures, is the legacy of the psychodrama of the Oedipus complex, its irresolution in childhood still pressing on the adult psyche. To some, this contribution to criminology or forensics – that an innocent person commits a crime because she feels guilty – might seem a typically wild psychoanalytic proposition. One can but reiterate that the emotions around the Oedipus complex are so protean, and feel so dangerous and potentially fatal to someone – if not everyone – in the triangle, that any displacement or discharge is attended by relief. Consider this story.

A man in flight from the police seeks sanctuary in a church. He enters the confessional and tells the priest he has just committed murder. The priest asks him when he was last in Confession, and what has led him to murder. He replies that one day, when he was a boy, he had torn apart a butterfly. He didn't know why he had done it, but as soon as he had, he felt so bad, so ashamed, so guilty, that he went to Confession. But the priest just said 'Butterflies don't count'. He was so shocked and horrified by this doctrinal decriminalisation of his act of violence, that he felt he had no bearings; and his guilt was still knotted within him. He decided never to go to church again.[18]

It may be wondered, with scepticism or scorn, whether the kid was a Nietzschean 'pale criminal'. The crucial point is that even he knew he was destroying, for whatever conscious or unconscious reason, something he had identified as beautiful and perhaps also good: he hadn't chosen to destroy a cockroach or a petri dish of bacteria. Some Freudians would find here further confirmation of their belief that the sense of beauty is a transform of libido. It is the melding of beauty and desire and need and violence and fear that returns us to the Oedipal realm. Interestingly, having destroyed the butterfly (mother, or is it father?), the boy doesn't go to either of his parents but to the superfather, the priest, that agent of the Highest Father.

At the heart of the Freudian project is the

seminal idea of the 'unconscious', a realm without time or negation or contradiction. The pressure of the unconscious upon the conscious does strange things to our conscious experience of intention and explanation. 'Inside the neurosis', writes Wollheim, 'desire, belief, and action are so concatenated that there is no interaction between the neurosis and reality: in that none of the outer manifestations of the neurosis are directed upon reality, nor are any of its internal constituents ever tested against reality'.[19] In the other case material brought by the Stoned Man, better known as the Rat Man, Freud showed that, contrary to the familiar Reality Principle understanding of the way belief and desire produce action (functionally/instrumentally), the Rat Man's almost ritualistic actions and desires – studying late to impress his father or examining his penis to defy him – were generated and constructed to sustain the false belief that his father, long-dead, was alive.[20]

The Unbecoming Mourning Girl

In 'Mourning and Melancholia', Freud distinguishes between the guilt of the bereaved and the shamelessness of the melancholic. The self-hating disposition 'induced' in the bereft woman is seen as a strategy to contain her unbearable guilt over her desperate rage at the lost person. The melancholic knows his wound is different from that of the bereft. A perfect expression of this disposition is given in Shakespeare's *The Merchant of Venice*:

In sooth I know not why I am so sad.
It wearies me, you say it wearies you . . .
. . . I have much ado to know myself.
(I, i, 1–2, 7)

The sense of not knowing the cause allows the parading of the wound. It becomes one's dress, one's persona. Some commentators have made the interpretation – which others see as culturally or anthropologically perilous – that Antonio's melancholy is the discharge of his barely conscious, and culturally illegal, homosexual love for Bassanio. Less controversially, one might state Freud's distressing truth:

A man who doubts his own love may, or rather ***must****, doubt every lesser thing.*[21]

(Freud's emphasis, but note the modal verbs!) The melancholic does not feel guilt or shame, because his sensations have not crystallised into desires and concepts that can be appraised. Perhaps he seeks a present rejection or attack to which he might give a more ordinary sensation-binding response, *viz.* an ordinary emotion. Despite his modish black dress, he is a very pale criminal.

We have seen Freud trace the presence of some varieties of guilt:

i. The partly personal, partly vicarious guilt of the Running Wife.

ii. The guilt at the impulse of hate, within ordinary ambivalence, of the Rat Man.

iii. The boundless guilt of the irresolved Oedipal complex, aching for the relief of present mundane transgression: the Pale Criminal.

iv. The longing of the melancholic for unknowingness to ground as guilt.

To these varieties of individual guilt, Freud – in his anthropological/sociological mode – added the notion of collective guilt. Human society and so human history begins, it is conjectured, with a brutal, reactive murder. Feeling frustrated and individually thwarted by the strongest male's monopolisation of the females in the primal horde, the remaining males unite to kill him, after which they also eat him. But they are surprised to find that the moment this is achieved, they feel a sense of guilt, individual and collective. This emotion prompts the memory of other emotions for the 'Father', such as love. In response to these, they institute certain taboos and rules which will avoid the repetition of such a murder and facilitate equal and safe opportunities for the fulfilment of the desires of each and every one of them.[22]

Taking this narrative as one parameter, Freud took contemporary Vienna as another. In *Civilisation and Its Discontents* (1930), he observed that the human cost of (high) civilisation, in terms of instinctual repression, was great; and when it became neurosis and psychosis, it was too great. Unlike some social theorists, Freud felt that all political (and religious) doctrines and ideologies would fail to deliver the happy society of happy individuals: whatever the classes or the resolution of the class-struggle, even a Stateless civil society would exact from its citizens the burden of some neuroses. The principal distinction was, and is, that the economically exploited classes have least access to the pleasant fruits of civilisation – the arts and the conversation about the arts.

Putting aside the questions of the historical validity and the explanatory force of Freud's conjectures, but not forgetting that cannibalism, mild or extreme, is always in present history, one might make the less controversial observation that societies find it very hard to remember and talk about their origins. (Perhaps it is too neat to say that in this they are exactly like Freud's ordinary neurotic who can't remember his infantile sexuality and infantile rage.) On the one hand, there are the epic narratives of the heroic establishment of societies sanctioned by divinities, Aeneas and Abraham. On the other hand, one might examine the amoral, temporal realm of the film *McCabe and Mrs Miller*.[23] Here, the hopefully-named American frontier town, Presbyterian Church, is in reality a place of Hobbesian struggle, degradation and murderous exploitation that its Minister must wink at. Progress is marked by a whore persuading an adventurer to relocate the other whores (which he provided for the labourers) from their tents on the plains – not so very different plains from Troy or Sinai – to a purpose-built brothel. In the symbolic, climactic scene, the Minister is shot in his church and it catches fire. We are left to conjecture – on the basis of the familiar forgetting of our present societies – that by the time the church is rebuilt in stone, not only will the brothel have gone, but the memory of it also. This naïve historical rewriting is also transparent in that post-wartime consolation-narrative, *It's A Wonderful Life*, where, in a fantasy scene, a divine agent shows the good Everyman, James

Stewart, the ugly city that his lifelong self-abnegating impulses have forestalled.[24]

See Melanie Play: Klein's Account of Guilt

Only sickness and age constrained Freud's desire to explore all the areas of the terrain he had marked out for his new paradigm. Melanie Klein is the first great theorist of the nursery. Her work stands on two pillars, both unsettling for the modern mind:

i. *All the sufferings of later life are for the most part repetitions of these early ones, and* ***every child in the first years of its life goes through an immeasurable degree of suffering.***[25] [my emphasis]

ii. ***I do not believe in the existence of a child in whom the capacity for love cannot be brought out.***[26] [Klein's emphasis]

This capacity, Klein believed, is tied to an intrinsic

sense of guilt that prompts reparation. Though the depravities of the 20th century have persuaded people to rethink their belief in the 'absolute innocence' of children, there is still the cherished hope that if external pressure on the family dyad or triad is lessened by societal and social provision, then children will be spared much unhappiness. In dissenting from this, and positing an ineluctable psychodrama between mother and child, Klein is accused of being ahistorical and pessimistic. We will return to this criticism. Given Klein's affirmation of the theoretical worth of the death-drive, the second quote above seems, surprisingly, to be a reinstitution of the Pelagian heresy which denies original sin and implies an inherent good that mortals – by free will alone, without divine grace – can manifest. Enlightenment liberals might find this reassuring still, but postmodernists and relativists are against any such *a priori* categorising.

We saw above that Freud believed in the resolution of the Oedipus complex by the establishment of the Superego, the guardian of the line of guilt, which happens at the ages of four to five.

Klein suggested that this form of resolution marked the 'zenith' of a process that had begun much earlier, in the first year of life. Here is her version. She posits that the child is programmed to relate, but that its first relations are with parts-of-persons, *viz*. objects; and the very first is with the breast. The ego-less baby imagines that its desires create the warm-breast which nourishes her. When she has had a satisfying feed, she designates the breast as a Good Object; but when the feed is unsatisfying or absent, she designates it as a Bad Object, which is frustrating and attacking her. Sometimes this frustration at the breast intensifies to the point where the baby feels unmanageable rage, or worse still, the primal terror of a sense of total disintegration. She tries to manage these feelings by projecting them into the Bad Breast, by using the mouth and anus as means of evacuation or as weapons of attack. This strategy brings relief until the baby realises that the Bad Breast, with her rage imposed on it, may retaliate and annihilate her. Klein calls this splitting and fear of the Object the 'paranoid-schizoid position'.

Gradually, the baby realises that she didn't create the breast, and that the breast is a single entity which is part of a person – a not-me Other-person – who loves her because she gives her good feeds. When the baby remembers her rages, she feels guilty and desolate that these might have damaged this person who loves her. This sadness and pining Klein calls the 'depressive position'. It is when the baby sees her mother continuing to be well and to be concerned for her that she realises she hasn't hurt her mother irreparably, and that they can have a mutually healthy relationship.

Freud placed the process of the establishment of the Superego at a point where the child has some facility for verbal communication, a facility that can ameliorate the aggression that provides the energy for the process. Despite this, in some children it seemed that their Superego – their psychic parent – was more strict and punishing than their actual parents. In moving this developmental sequence to the first year of life, a significantly less verbal stage, Klein saw the child at the mercy of frustrations which released his aggressive and destructive instincts to the point where they became unmanageable, with little hope of these sensations being bound into emotion and thought by language. Thus the stakes seemed that much higher: the infant/child's need to evacuate or project his hatred, and his subsequent fear of the 'lost' projected hatred homing in on him, were all the more powerful.

They were dreading a cruel retaliation from their parents as a punishment for their aggressive phantasies directed against those parents . . . unconsciously, expecting to be cut to pieces, beheaded, devoured and so on . . . [27]

We are now a long way from Wordsworth's uncomplicated, innocent child. But Klein was able to support these terrifying conjectures through her incredibly extensive observations and detailed case notes on the play of her young patients.

Unsurprisingly, she came to similar conclusions as Freud about the idea of criminality; that the persistently naughty child is perhaps trying to use conscious, present wrongdoing, with its predictable punishments, as a way of lessening a deeply unconscious sense of guilt and anxiety over barely remembered displays of aggression. Such children 'would feel compelled to be naughty and to get punished, because the real punishment, however severe, was reassuring in comparison with the murderous attacks which they were continually expecting from fantastically cruel parents'.[28]

These ideas, and those of Wilfred Bion, Klein's greatest disciple, seem on first acquaintance even wilder and more repellent than Freud's. And yet they provide a conceptual framework that can help one understand a variety of strange phenomena: the slide from emotional deprivation to moral depravity of torturers and murderers, as in Henry Dick's *Licensed Mass Murder*; the *frisson* of fear watching the gestation of the eponymous *Alien*; and also latency-period sexuality as portrayed in the Spanish film, *The Tit and the Moon*, in which a young boy responds to the advent of a baby brother with a generalised fascination with the breasts of his mother and of all the women in the town.[29]

It is important to remember that Klein talks of 'positions', not 'phases'. So one's lifelong psychodrama will consist of an ineluctable, and irrepressible, pendular movement between the paranoid-schizoid and the depressive positions. The intensity of one's first experiences at these positions will give one an internal reference point for later repetitions.

Any pain caused by unhappy experiences, whatever their nature, has something in common with mourning. It reactivates the infantile depressive position; the encountering and overcoming of adversity of any kind entails mental work similar to mourning.[30]

In childhood, the depressive position had repaired, even 'brought back to life', the internal Good figures that the child felt she had almost fatally damaged. Though in later life the Other, whether kin or friend, is actually dead, the ordinary mourner still needs to establish the aliveness of her memories and the Other's presence in her ego.

The melancholic is distinguished by his inability to do this: he just goes bleating on and on.

Psychoanalytic theory contains very few statements concerning health – the criteria for individual mental well-being and for mutually fulfilling social relations. One such is in Klein's great paper, 'Love, Guilt and Reparation'. Here, she reiterates her core beliefs:

At the bottom our strongest hatred, however, is directed against the hatred within ourselves. Feelings of guilt are a fundamental incentive towards creativeness and work in general (even of the simplest kinds).[31]

Perhaps if Freud had had time to be in the nursery longer, he would have felt, like Klein, compelled to observe:

I must say that the impression I get of the way in which even the quite small child fights his unsocial tendencies is rather touching and impressive.[32]

And perhaps it is only when women and men have

children of their own, and experience the strangely puzzling phenomenon of the seemingly boundless rage and despair of little children, that they understand finally the necessary yet ordinary parental and human tasks of the containment and holding of human distress.

Stop Making Sense: Other Voices

Freud and Klein set the broad terrain of the psychoanalytic meaning of guilt. In this section I will introduce 'shame', the concept often connected with guilt. I will defend the idea of internalisation that both concepts require to explain their origin and abiding force, and I will describe how the five basic physical senses are attached to them.

Guilt is usually confused with shame, and both are sometimes subsumed under barely specific 'anxiety'. When one remembers that even animals (as well as infants) feel anxiety, one realises that some other experience or faculty must be present in guilt and shame. It is a moot point whether animals feel shame and guilt. Though their beloved beasts look shameful and guilty to pet owners and farmers, this seems more like a human social construct. After all, 'bad' pigs and dogs are no longer tried and hung as they were until a couple of centuries back. The human capacity for these emotions is based on the faculty of internalisation.

What is internalised may be something initially external, or it may be an introjection of something initially projected out; and the 'thing' is a force, or an object, a part-object, or a self. Old English caught this idea perfectly in the phrase defining remorse, 'agenbite of inwit': 'remorse of conscience'.[33] 'In this cannibalistic encounter who is biting whom?', asks Aldous Huxley.

The creditable aspects of the self bite the discreditable and are themselves bitten, receiving wounds that fester with incurable shame and despair.[34]

No one would question the experiential accuracy of the sensation of biting. Just as hunger seems to be an internal 'biting', so is remorse. Perhaps the objection is to the idea of 'selves' – that it is too sophisticated a concept for a young child.

We could say that psychoanalysis proposes three levels of mentation: plain thinking, daydreaming and unconscious phantasy. Some emotional affect is tied to each, but that attached to phantasy is the least accessible to consciousness. Consider this mother's story about a visit to the Body Zone at the Millennium Dome: 'Putting my three year old to bed that night, she asked me, "Mum, do I have escalators in my legs?"'[35] Now, at the level of actual (shared) reality, at the shopping mall and the tube station, the little girl can think, compare, how *big* escalators are and how *little* are her legs. From these and from the concept of 'toy', she might have daydreamed, even before visiting the Dome, about a big doll body, so big that one would need ladders or escalators to get to the top, inside or out. But her thought – and this is what connects it to *phantasy* – is that she *might* have escalators *inside* her legs. But in this phantasy the idea of *agency* is in suspense, for she *knows* she can't 'get on' her own legs. Nor can her own legs 'get on' her, for where is the 'her' that her legs could get on? The phantasy shows her trying to make sense of the puzzle of 'willed motion', and beyond this, the criteria for 'aliveness'. This child has negotiated the dangers of alexthymia – being or feeling unable to find or use words – and performed a very complex linguistic, conceptual and psychological operation. She has taken something in: it is, at its most rudimentary, an idea of a force over which she has no control, but which – crucially – she has given a shape and a name. It is possible that if this child had already done some work on this fundamental puzzle, what she was doing with her remark was being playful with her mum.

Here, we are back at the boundary that psychoanalysis has dared to claim and explore. What bridges the distance between the three year old (and there may be even more precocious two year olds minting such phantasies) and the 'unverbal' six-month infant, is precisely the unconscious – or, in a contemporary metamorphosis, 'the unthought known'.[36]

Most people would say that shame is both a

more awful and a less awful experience than guilt. This, again, is because of the 'where' that it is experienced. 'Shame is the Cinderella of the unpleasant emotions, having received much less attention than anxiety, guilt and depression', writes Rycroft, prompting in me the trivial fantasy of what her magical glass slipper would symbolise.[37] Erikson explains this insufficient attention as arising from the fact that 'in our civilisation it [shame] is so early and easily absorbed by guilt'.[38] But at least he accords it a stage – the second, and taking place in infancy – in his developmental account of the eight dichotomies to be negotiated in a human life. He pairs it with 'doubt', and contrasts them both with 'autonomy', the attainment of a sense of integrity, skill and self-sufficient power with regard to primary bodily functions – eating and excretion. Shame is the sensation consequent upon the exposure of failed autonomy or hubris. The audience is one's mother/parent, one's status reference group, one's Superego, or one's Ego-Ideal. Imagine yourself at a posh dinner, eating pea and tarragon soup. If your hand slips, your bib will turn green and your face red – and red and green must never be seen! But what if a pea falls in your cleavage – oh, Princess, what colour then!

These shameful displays are visible to the fumbler and to the audience. There is a worse humiliation, captured by the common expression 'to have egg on one's face', when the fumbling eater can't see the debris of his clumsiness, and the shame is worse because the Egg Man must now relive all the possibilities of having been seen, from the breakfast table to the workplace. But the front of the body which *hasn't* been seen reminds one of the back of the body which *can't* be seen. It is the literal and metaphoric difficulty of the sense of a behind, to do with faeces, the past, and leaving the unseeable, which inspires Erikson's wonderful aphorism, 'Doubt is the brother of shame'.[39] A parent's ambivalence about having a child will take one form with respect to difficulties in feeding that child; but a different intensity will attend difficulties with anal training. From the child's point of view, writes Erikson, 'from a sense of loss of self-control and of foreign overcontrol comes a lasting propensity for doubt and shame'.[40]

It is at the next developmental stage that 'guilt' is introduced, forming the negative of the dichotomous pair with 'initiative'. The guilt here is once again the nameless residue of the Oedipal situation. What the child must relinquish is the desire to know its mother's body, transforming it into a desire to know the non-mother world. As Erikson says, 'Visual shame precedes auditory guilt, which is a sense of badness to be had all by oneself when nobody watches and when everything is quiet except the voice of the Superego'.[41] One's eyes can't see themselves without the mirror of another's eyes, and – tragically – one's lips can't kiss themselves; but one can hear, both with the 'inner' and 'outer' ears, the commands that one speaks to oneself. From this phenomenon, Isakower argued that the Superego derives from the auditory sphere.[42] It seems to be the defining quality of shame that it is brief, whereas guilt is enduring. For Sartre, Hell is a place where one can't turn out the light.[43]

Another fundamental point in connection with shame and guilt is an anthropological one – the distinction between 'shame cultures' and 'guilt cultures'. Examples of the former include Japan and Pakistan (about which Salman Rushdie wrote his novel *Shame*); and of the latter, any Western country – though within these there may be shame-bound subcultures like the military. These are human, social constructs, and the crucial factor is who is in the in-group. Perhaps guilt and shame are a zero-sum pair, so that in any given culture more shame means less guilt. Nina Colthart, an English analyst who converted to Buddhism, could declare in a tone more believable than Adrian Mole's, 'I do not feel guilt'.[44]

The sense that is least theorised is smell. Freud made the enlightening point that when *Homo sapiens* became upright, the now greater distance between the anus and genitalia and the nose altered the value of smell. Strict clinical practices and religious rituals were instituted to deal with the feared meaning of the smell of menses and smegma and faeces. Even contemporary cultures differ in where the line of an unacceptable smell is drawn. It is the least controllable and, perhaps because of this, the most powerfully affecting sense when it 'invades' consciousness – remember the smell of school soap, your pet's fur, your first kiss . . . ? But can one smell shame or guilt?

It is a commonplace that one can smell fear, and that animals can smell it better than humans. Human fear is at its most intense in a duel, the unsupported battle, and in a physical, hands-on duel-dyad such as boxing. Just before the climax of a boxing match, there is a strange homoerotic embrace, when the combatants can smell, feel and taste blood, sweat and perhaps even tears – but certainly fear. Perhaps the fear is prompted by a sudden awareness of a sense of puzzlement: 'What am I doing here? Whose fight is it? What is its meaning? What would victory mean?' The person who gets past this moment wins – he can effect the necessary separation with a consciousness-shattering blow to the other.

So what is the meaning of such fights, and the meaning of the hesitation before the killer blow?

Perhaps humans sense in that hesitation the fear of unmanageable guilt at attaining the forbidden: a fear of the stench of sin poisoning the sweet scent of victory. It might seem another typically wild psychoanalytic conjecture to suggest that boxing contains a recrudescence of the primal horde. Given the theoretical primacy of the Oedipus complex, it is interesting that there are, in reality, very few narratives of fathers and sons fighting. There seems to be an asymmetry in the sense of a right to self-defence in the fight between fathers and sons. The son knows intuitively that he needs the father to be alive to give him a self he can defend and live with. So one might conjecture that in the stand-off between the unhappily named Gayes, the preacher-father felt he could shoot, while his songwriting son Marvin, even at 44, felt no equivalent permission. The latter's recent top-selling single had been 'Sexual Healing'! After the filiacide, Marvin's mother (whose own father had shot her mother), lamented: 'For some reason, my husband didn't love Marvin and, what's worse, he didn't want me to love Marvin either. Marvin wasn't very old before he understood that.' His sister added: 'I have no doubt that this is exactly how Marvin chose to die. He punished Father, by making certain that the rest of his life would be miserable.'[45]

The limiting case of reaction-formation, when a person manages a terrifying desire by acting out the opposite desire, is the troubled child's fantasy of saving his father's life. This is illustrated perfectly in the film *Back to the Future*. The young man of the 1980s is stranded in the 1950s, the time of his parents' youth. He sees his father as a dorky 'wuss' humiliated by the class neanderthals. At this point he hesitates about helping; but later, when his father falls in front of a car, he leaps forward – saving his dad's life and, with the impact of the car, losing consciousness.[46] Because the teenage boy (unlike the air-fighting kid) has arrived at moral consciousness, he would realise that even this action would not allow him a guiltless life.

Is such hesitation the last vestige of Oedipal rage? Several million readers and critics have tried to give the definitive explanation for that perfect narrative of hesitation, *Hamlet*. T.S. Eliot famously initiated the Copernican shift when he questioned its perfection, calling it 'an artistic failure' and introducing into the language that haunting phrase, '[absence of] objective correlative'.[47] At about this time, his co-writer of the Hogarth stable, Freud, was puzzling over exactly this – the fact that the child's Superego does not correlate with the objective level of kindness or threat from its parents. The child feels, of course, an absolute sense of objective, psychic reality: the awareness of an unmanageable burden of desire, guilt, shame and fear within him/her, even if no one else can see or confirm it. So it is that Hamlet can say to his uncomprehending 'friends', Rosencrantz and Guildenstern, in absolute truth:

O God, I could be bounded in a nutshell and count myself a king of infinite space, were it not that I have bad dreams. (II, ii, 258–60)

It is because he sees those dreams/phantasies made flesh – and ugly, sex-smelling flesh – in his uncle, that he hesitates over killing him, for that would be more like suicide! Even when he says 'Now could I drink hot blood' (III, ii, 398), he is still only a thought away from being paralysed by sophistry born of unconscious guilt. At the least, Freud's suggestion, unlike Eliot's theory, preserves one's absolute awe at the play.

Displacement is a key idea in psychoanalysis. Once his Oedipal hatred is displaced onto his uncle, Hamlet is stuck again. In this final example, I want to show how guilt can be so intense and protean that once the sense to which it is tied becomes manageable, it gets displaced onto a sense that is not manageable. A strange 'synaesthesia' happens in this realm, not merely like 'hearing' colours, but where one's anxiety about the uncertainty of one sense is heightened by the intense awareness of another sense.

Freud introduces Lady Macbeth as a perfect exemplar of the phenomenon he names as 'Wrecked By Success'.[48] (Today's adolescents, 18–30, would define success as having the financial means to be wrecked by drink, drugs and sex whenever one wanted. And yet even among their heroes, the appetites may pall, bringing the depression known as 'Paradise Syndrome' – a recent sufferer being Dave Stewart of The Eurythmics.) The attainment of Lady Macbeth's desires seems to release an unconscious and utterly unmanageable (Oedipal) guilt which not only casts a shadow over her enjoyment of the fruits of success – queenly power – but almost compels her to suicide as a form of atonement.

When, at the beginning, she reads the witches' prophecy and knows Duncan is coming, she 'prays':

Come, you spirits
That tend on mortal thoughts, unsex me here . . .
Come to my woman's breasts,
And take my milk for gall, you murd'ring ministers.
(I, v, 40–1, 47–8)

This is a rare example of a person wishing for some external force to do the work of projection. She is certain that she can't see these beings, in their 'sightless substances'. At the murder scene, her bravado collapses at a perspective/gestalt, a shape-shift, of Duncan's face that she had not registered during the hours of feasting just ended. (It is said that the shapes one can't see immediately in some dual-perspective puzzles reveal one's anxieties.)

Had he not resembled
My father as he slept, I had done't. (II, ii, 12–13)

Despite being unsexed and half drunk, she can't use the (penile) daggers to penetrate Duncan's flesh: she daren't even touch the body of the father.

After the murder, Macbeth longs for blindness and can barely let go of the daggers – he stands paralysed. The deed done, Lady Macbeth has enough manic energy to see the dead Duncan and to 'refute' Macbeth's misperception that the blood he has spilled would stain oceans: 'I shame to wear a heart so white . . . A little water clears us of this deed.' (II, ii, 63–4, 66) Macbeth, however, has taken in the idea of an indelible stain. The fact of the absence of the stain in the real world leads to a synaesthesia: visual absence becomes a sense of an enduring silence always about to be shattered by sound, the sound of the external world, the sound of judgement. By the end of the play, Lady Macbeth is seeing something that isn't there: the spots of blood from 17 years earlier. Before Bodyform towels gave women the 'power' to fly and swim, it was precisely spots of (menstrual) blood which revealed the womanliness of the woman trying to unsex herself, like Pope Joan or Teena Brandon.[49] For Macbeth, the synaesthesia is from sight to sound and touch; for Lady Macbeth, it is to smell:

Yet who would have thought the old man to have had so much blood in him. . . . Here's the smell of blood still. All the perfumes of Arabia will not sweeten this little hand. Oh, oh, oh! (V, i, 41–2, 52–4)

In her sleepwalking she is invisible to herself, and in this blindness she falls to her death, and release. We are to understand that her being stuck at smell is an index of her weaker moral capacity. Macbeth comes to understand his moral collapse in a way she never does. I don't know if this would have any diagnostic value – asking criminals which sense was ascendant at what age, and which during the crime?

The voice of guilt is like a maddening, trashy pop song – unstoppable, a loop, a Laingian Knot.[50]

Jill feels guilty
that Jack feels guilty
that Jill feels guilty
that Jack feels guilty.

***He** feels that he is unhappy because he is guilty to be happy when others are unhappy and that he made a mistake to marry someone who can only think of happiness.*

It can be worse, as Laing knew, for a man with less than 'six degrees of separation' from the Thane of Glamis:

Jimmy McKenzie was a bloody pest at the mental

hospital because he went around shouting back at his voices. We could only hear one end of the conversation, of course, but the other end could be inferred in general terms at least from: 'Away tae fuck, ye filthy-minded bastards . . .'[51]

What kind of physic, what kind of therapy would help poor Jimmy?

Speak Up Ye Buggers! Start Making Sense: Therapy

It was decided at one and the same time to alleviate his distress and ours, by giving him the benefit of a leucotomy. An improvement in his condition was noted. After the operation he went around no longer shouting abuse at his voices, but: 'What's that? Say that again! Speak up ye buggers, I cannae hear ye!'[52]

The advent of the leucotomy made actual what for Macbeth and Shakespeare, centuries earlier, had been a fantasy of healing. Like Laing's modern

Everyman Jack, above, Macbeth as king feels guilty for having been part of the cause of the monumental burden of guilt that his wife carries. In one of his most tender speeches, Macbeth asks the doctor:

Canst thou not minister to a mind diseased,
Pluck from the memory a rooted sorrow,
Raze out the written troubles of the brain,
And with some sweet oblivious antidote
Cleanse the stuff'd bosom of that perilous stuff
Which weighs upon the heart? (V, iii, 40–5)

This can stand as a prophetic misconception of the way psychoanalysis works. Interestingly, this is the most famous doctor of medicine in Shakespeare and, within this play, there is the powerful contrast between his inability and the almost mystical powers of healing of the English king. There is not space within this book for a detailed discussion of the way therapy works. The obvious can be restated: therapy provides the space for barely-remembered and unmanageable thoughts and feelings to find words and gestures and to be discussed in such a way that they can be transcended and forgotten healthily. And again, the therapist does not see her task as involving a quasi-priestly or quasi-warden role, as defined by contemporary paradigms, religious or political. These facets of guilt are attended to by the State and the Church. A person may go willingly to a confessor and religiously perform penitential tasks; and he may go willingly to prison and comply with the penitentiary requirements, stated and implied. But after these, he may still feel a residue of unconscious guilt.

Even seemingly ordinary, good people may feel troubled. I came home to find that my housemate, who is hardly ever in the house long enough to produce dirt, had cleaned the toilet and bathroom, even polished the taps. 'Oh, thank you so much', I said. 'I don't do enough', he said. 'You do more than enough', I replied. 'It doesn't help', he said, in a strangely tragic tone. I was surprised, and said with some hesitation: 'Is it guilt?' 'Yes', he said, and again in such a sad tone that I felt we should speak no more about it.

This is the realm of psychoanalysis. Its right to this realm is still challenged by religion and other paradigms – and specifically for a certain range of symptoms such as obsessive-compulsive disorder. The abbreviation OCD for this condition (which Freud had long dissected) was first popularised by Rapoport, the title of whose book used a typical symptom: *The Boy Who Couldn't Stop Washing*. Such a symptom isn't merely the product of better plumbing! The idea of an intense, ineluctable guilt was captured millennia past by the idea of 'scrupulosity'. Freud saw such symptoms of repetition as ways of managing unmanageable sensations/emotions like anxiety and guilt. Rapoport dissents from this explanation, citing research which shows the inadequacy of psychoanalysis to alleviate such symptoms. Her ethological conclusion is that the primal instinct for some ordinary activity such as cleanliness in nest-building and nest-living has gone chemically wrong, and that the best therapeutic strategy is drug-based.[53]

A sense of guilt is therefore not privileged, in

terms of theory or technique, as the primary symptom to be attended to.

It was Freud's colleague Josef Breuer's inability to cope, as a man, with his patient's desire for him as a complex man, sexually and emotionally available now and to her, rather than a man defined by a single professional role predicated on an almost object-like abstinence, which prompted Freud to reconsider these emotional dynamics and to place at the heart of the psychoanalytic process the concepts of 'transference' and 'counter-transference'.[54] The past must come into the present, into the therapeutic space, as powerfully as it can – and that can only be by the 'misperceptions' of transference, if there is to be a new future, rather than endless, futile shadow-repetition. In the re-creation of powerful thoughts and feelings that transference facilitates, there is the hope that the patient might (be helped to) complete or at least continue the transition from what Klein calls the paranoid-schizoid position to the depressive position. These are the most painful sessions, whatever one's age. Klein held the analytic (if not the received motherly) line when she wrote: 'This is done in analysis only through purely analytic measures, not at all by advising or encouraging the child.'[55]

To remind the reader of the contrast, one might quote from the Hebrew ritual to relieve scrupulosity: 'May everything be permitted you, may everything be forgiven you, may everything be allowed you.'[56] This seems a curious tense – the intercessionary subjunctive – showing once more the complexities of the grammar of the human heart. A different reference point is the wonderfully cynical strapline in *House of Cards*, in which the devious Minister often leaks assent by replying: '*You* might think that: I couldn't *possibly* comment!'[57] Some may argue that the therapeutic emotional abstinence which intends to be non-directive and facilitating might become manipulative in this way.

The renewed interest in psychoanalysis during the 1960s was coincidental with the so-called 'permissive society', one of the howling misnomers of that century of language abuse. There was no genuine, intergenerational dialogue, closing with the benign granting of permission. No parental blessings were offered, just the implicit curses of sullen silence and resentment, or 'guilt-trips' as they were called.

The distinction between psychodynamic and non-psychodynamic therapies is of the same order as the difference in potential emotional charge between live theatre and the cinema. In his great paper, 'Hate In The Counter-Transference', Donald Winnicott examines the pressures, internal and external, that the therapist must manage and use.[58] This is not to deny the worth of non-psychodynamic therapies. And, of course, the patient in non-psychodynamic therapy isn't watching a film of a therapist – the simple point of difference is that he/she will be, on the basis of theory and technique, trying to abstract out, control, disinhibit, 'over'-contain, transferential dynamics. Psychodynamic therapists might suspect that in such other therapies, though seemingly guiltless knowledge and behaviour are arrived at, the heart or psyche may still feel fundamentally broken by guilt.

Roll Away the Stone: Final Thoughts

Where does the debate about guilt in psychoanalysis go from here? The disciplines of anthropology and sociology invite connection.

a.) A Ruthless Computation of the Forces

The Homeric heroes knew nothing of that cumbersome word ***responsibility****, nor would they have believed in it if they had. For them, it was as if every crime were committed in a state of mental infirmity. But such infirmity meant that a god was present and at work. . . . For [them] there was no guilty party, only guilt, immense guilt. . . . With an intuition the moderns have jettisoned and have never recovered, the heroes did not distinguish between the evil of the mind and the evil of the deed, murder and death. Guilt for them is like a boulder blocking the road; it is palpable, it looms. Perhaps the guilty party is as much a sufferer as the victim. In confronting guilt, all we can do is make a ruthless computation of the forces involved.*[59]

How wonderful that the metaphor Calasso chooses for guilt, in his sublime meditation on Greek mythology, should be the same as that of Freud's Rat Man. And there is another perfect coincidence of these great Hellenists. The above quote displays the guilt attached to mighty political actions. But guilt is also lodged in something ordinary, diurnal and utterly essential.

The primordial crime is the action that makes something in existence disappear: the act of eating. Guilt is thus obligatory and inextinguishable. . . . The gods aren't content to foist guilt on man. That wouldn't be enough, since guilt is part of life always. What the gods demand is an awareness of guilt. And this can only be achieved through sacrifice.[60]

There have been, and there remain, many different social formations. And one might ask questions like: Do arranged-marriage cultures privilege the mother-son relationship in such a way that the Oedipus complex is significantly attenuated? But despite the experiential fact of psychic bisexuality, each individual learns to live as one gender, with its allowed powers and attendant terrors. Perhaps it is male fear and womb-envy which provide the best explanation for the literary-anthropological puzzle: Why is Isaac saved, but not Iphigenia? Some argue that it is the male bias, even within psychoanalysis, which has led to the under-use of the term 'Elektra complex'. If the primary triangle is the source of psychoanalytic guilt, then the specificity of women's experience of this triangle must be honoured.

I am mindful, as a male, that the concepts 'female masochism', 'eroticisation of female self-hatred' and 'female violence' need to be theorised more subtly. The way in which a culture situates a woman's moral right to a violent impulse or a violent response will determine her psychological sense of this right, and the attendant guilt she is expected to feel. Any shift in this 'ideology' will affect, within three generations, the formation of the Superego of the children to come. In the West, if not yet in the East, there is a debate about whether there can be gender-blind definitions of 'provocation' and thus of legal responsibility and moral guilt. One cannot imagine, in any century before the 20th, a woman publishing a book entitled *Eve was Framed*.[61] The Greek myths didn't blame Helen.

These recent conceptual revaluations, such as the delineation of 'date rape' and the redefinition of 'abuse' after Cleveland, throw their tragic light on past narratives, but also a more hopeful light upon the future. They also affect one's reading of texts: most recently the Sylvia Plath–Ted Hughes controversies. It is worth recalling that even *the* dramatist, writing when a queen was ascendant, did not write 'enough' on the mother-daughter relationship. There are no mothers in Shakespeare's great comedies, but many fathers and daughters. Why?

b.) Taking the Group Seriously

Some, like Dalal, the title of whose book is taken as the heading for this subsection, would say that this is the next theoretical challenge: 'to build bridges between psychoanalysis and sociology.'[62] He is inspired by the phrase in Freud's account of the resolution of the Oedipus complex: '*Ideologies* of the Superego' (his emphasis).[63] Though one might concur with his questioning of the theoretical and moral worth of a monolithic individualism, the question remains: In what way does a group *need* other groups? Freud observed an 'inclination to aggression' that humans 'do not feel comfortable without'; and also that despised subgroups, like Jews, 'rendered most useful services to their hosts'.[64] But as the internecine warfare among the Christian States (of 'universal love') shows us, one 'enemy' isn't enough.

Out of the unprecedented barbarities of the last century, both at the level of the hearth and the State, has come the idea of 'the impassability of the Other': to make disappear the hope and right to flourish of another individual or another culture is an action requiring a sense of absolute guilt.

Murder and war are justified by the belief of scarcity, whether born of reality, imagination or greed. The baby, believing the breast she needs may not be enough, or may disappear, takes it all in, makes it disappear. The baby cannot imagine that others may be hungry. Later, there is the perfect developmental moment when the baby being fed turns the spoon to feed her feeder: she believes there is enough for all. Nations perennially fail to attain this moment. At one end of the global village are the self-famishing; at the other, the politically famished. Starving saves the labours of the sacrificial knife, and also prolongs guilt. All the G8 or dinner-table talk about the 'problem' of famine is just an evasion. Yes, it is hard to talk about such things – for but two thoughts away from consciousness is the terrifying realm of fearful guilt. For many, there is something absolutely unbearable about the whining special pleading of an Albert Speer or a Myra Hindley. Their monstrous mountains of text and talk, decades of it, didn't and don't produce even a squeaking mouse of believable understanding of guilt, let alone remorse, that would begin the dialogue of reconciliation. Perhaps their abiding ignorance and moral deformity is the effluence of society's perennial, messy and fruitless engagement of these fundamental concepts.

Coda

The impassability of the Other. Who believes this? It is known that perverts, however defined, do not usually come to therapy, and when they do, they do not wish to be 'cured', only to have their nagging guilt allayed. They say, 'Don't I have the right to do this?' The only answer is: 'It also depends on the right of the Other! And what does it mean that you can't allay your own guilt?'

So how many Others? Could this not also be an index of civilisation: the increasing range of possible actions of infringement of the Other that the mentally healthy individual, Seinfeld's 'whole new animal', should feel guilty about? But this kind of guilt would be based neither on a sense of sin nor a fear of punishment, so it would neither cripple the bearer nor harm the Other, but rather facilitate their genuine intimacy. In that index is the hope of good hesitation, that will slowly leaven the community and attenuate, generation upon generation, the 'bad' guilt that the Superego demands. Perhaps I should feel guilty in concluding that what the world needs is more guilt!

Acknowledgements

I would like to thank: Ivan Ward of the Freud Museum, for his generosity of spirit and lavish editorial attentions; Duncan Heath and Jeremy Cox, of Icon, for their steadying hands; my colleagues at Cambridge University Counselling Service for splendid supervision and support; and the following, whose affection is between the lines: François Danis, Dan Jones, Matthew Jones, Alan MacDonald, Dieter Peetz, Corinna Russell, Maggie Smith, and Wendy Thurley.

Dedication

For my parents:
Chanchal Singh Nannar and Jit Kaur Dhaliwal.

Notes

1. Townsend, S., *The Secret Diary of a Provincial Man: Adrian Mole*, in *The Guardian*, 15 January 2000.

2. Meade, M., *The Unruly Life of Woody Allen*, London: Weidenfeld and Nicolson, 2000.

3. Ibid.

4. The Bible: Exodus, 20:5.

5. Bruce, L., *The Essential Lenny Bruce*, London: Macmillan, 1972.

6. Goldhagen, D.J., *Hitler's Willing Executioners: Ordinary Germans and the Holocaust*, London: Little, Brown, 1996.

7. Seinfeld, J., *Seinfeld*, USA: Castle Rock Entertainment, 1998.

8. Apocryphal.

9. Linehan, G. and Mathews, A., *Hippies*, UK: BBC2, 1999.

10. Freud, S., *Inhibitions, Symptoms and Anxiety* (1925), London: Penguin Freud Library 10, 1979, p. 240.

11. Harrison, K., *The Kiss*, London: Fourth Estate, 1997, pp. 142–3.

12. Freud, S., letter to Fleiss (1899), quoted in Wollheim, R., *Freud*, London: Fontana, 1991, p. 120.

13. Freud, S., *Introductory Lectures* (1916), London: Penguin Freud Library 1, 1973, p. 301.

14. Ovid, *The Erotic Poems*, London: Penguin, 1982.

15. Kafka, F., *Letters to Felice*, London: Vintage, 1999, p. 547.

16. Freud, S., *A Case of Obsessional Neurosis: Rat Man* (1909), London: Penguin Freud Library 9, 1979, p. 70.

17. Freud, S., *Some Character-Types* (1916), London: Penguin Freud Library 14, 1985, p. 317.

18. *Butterflies Don't Count*, UK: BBC2, date uncertain.

19. Wollheim, R., *Freud*, London: Fontana, 1991, p. 137.

20. Freud, S., *Rat Man*, p. 84.

21. Ibid., p. 121.

22. Freud, S., *Totem and Taboo* (1912), London: Penguin Freud Library 13, 1985.

23. Altman, R., *McCabe and Mrs Miller*, USA: 1971.

24. Capra, F., *It's a Wonderful Life*, USA: 1946.

25. Klein, M., 'Criminal Tendencies in Normal Children' (1927), in *Love, Guilt and Reparation and Other Works, 1921–1945*, London: Vintage, 1988, p. 173.

26. Ibid., p. 184.

27. Klein, M., 'On Criminality' (1934), in Klein, op. cit., 1988, p. 258.

28. Ibid.

29. Dick, H.V., *Licensed Mass Murder*, London: 1972; Scott, R., *Alien*, UK: 1979; Luna, B., *The Tit and The Moon*, Spain: 1994.

30. Klein, M., 'Mourning' (1940), in Klein, op. cit., 1988, p 360.

31. Klein, M., 'Love, Guilt and Reparation' (1937), in Klein, op. cit., 1988, pp. 340, 335.

32. Klein, M., 'Criminal Tendencies in Normal Children' (1927), in Klein, op. cit., 1988, p. 176.

33. Joyce, J., *Ulysses* (1922); Joyce is quoting an old text.

34. Huxley, A., *The Perennial Philosophy*, London: Flamingo, 1946, p. 309.

35. Engle, C., letter to *The Guardian*, 8 February 2000.

36. Bollas, C., *The Shadow of the Object: Psychoanalysis of the Unthought Known*, London: Free Association Books, 1987.

37. Rycroft, C., *Dictionary of Psychoanalysis*, London: Penguin, 1968, p. 152.

38. Erikson, E., *Childhood and Society*, London: Paladin, 1963, p. 227.

39. Ibid., p. 228.

40. Ibid.

41. Ibid., p. 227.

42. Isakower, O., 'On the Exceptional Position of the Auditory Sphere', *International Journal of Psychoanalysis*, vol. 20, 1939.

43. Sartre, J.-P., *In Camera* (1944), London: Penguin, 1990.

44. Coltart, N., Freud Museum Conference, 1997, question time.

45. Ritz, D., *Divided Soul: Marvin Gaye*, London: Michael Joseph, 1985, pp. 7, 336.

46. Zemeckis, R., *Back to the Future*, USA: 1985.
47. Eliot, T.S., *'Hamlet'* (1919), in *Selected Prose*, London: Faber and Faber, 1975, p. 48.
48. Freud, S., *Some Character-Types* (1916), London: Penguin Freud Library 14, 1985, p. 299.
49. Apocryphal; Peirce, K., *Boys Don't Cry*, USA: 1999.
50. Laing, R.D., *Knots*, London: Penguin, 1970, pp. 26, 28.
51. Laing, R.D., *The Politics of Experience*, London: Penguin, 1967, p. 146.
52. Ibid.
53. Rapoport, J., *The Boy Who Couldn't Stop Washing*, London: Collins, 1990, p. 15.
54. Freud, S. and Breuer, J., *Studies on Hysteria* (1895), London: Penguin Freud Library 3.
55. Klein, M., 'Criminal Tendencies in Normal Children' (1927), in Klein, op. cit., 1988, pp. 176–7.
56. Rapoport, op. cit., 1990, p. 232.
57. Dobbs, M., *House of Cards*, London: Collins, 1989; BBC TV, 1990.
58. Winnicott, D., 'Hate In The Counter-Transference' (1947), in *Collected Papers*, London: Karnac, 1992.
59. Calasso, R., *The Marriage of Cadmus and Harmony* (1988), London: Vintage, 1994, p. 94.
60. Ibid., pp. 311–13.
61. Kennedy, H., *Eve Was Framed*, London: Vintage, 1993.

62. Dalal, F., *Taking the Group Seriously*, London: Jessica Kingsley, 1998, p. 121.

63. Ibid.

64. Freud, S., *Civilisation and Its Discontents* (1930), London: Penguin Freud Library 12, 1985, p. 305.

Further Reading

Appignanesi, R. and Zarate, O., *Introducing Freud*, Cambridge: Icon Books, 1999.

Calasso, R., *The Marriage of Cadmus and Harmony*, London: Vintage, 1994.

Clendinnen, I., *Reading the Holocaust*, Cambridge: Cambridge University Press, 1999.

Cox, M., (ed.), *Remorse and Reparation*, London: Jessica Kingsley, 1999.

Dalal, F., *Taking the Group Seriously*, London: Jessica Kingsley, 1998.

Freud, S., *Some Character-Types Met With in Psycho-analytic Work* (1916), London: Penguin Freud Library 14, 1985.

Hinshelwood, R., Robinson, S. and Zarate, O., *Introducing Melanie Klein*, Cambridge: Icon Books, 1999.

Klein, M., 'Criminal Tendencies in Normal Children' (1927), in Klein, M., *Love, Guilt and Reparation and Other Works, 1921–1945*, London: Vintage, 1988.

Schimmel, S., *The Seven Deadly Sins: Jewish, Christian and Classical Reflections on Human Psychology*, Oxford: Oxford University Press, 1992.

Ward, I., *Introducing Psychoanalysis*, Cambridge: Icon Books, 2000.